MY FIRST POCKET GUIDE

SEASHORE
LIFE

D0424641

Text/Consultant: Jenna Kinghorn
Illustrators: Evi Antoniou, Joanna Cameron, Simone End

Published by
The National Geographic Society
Reg Murphy, President and Chief Executive Officer
Gilbert M. Grosvenor, Chairman of the Board
Nina D. Hoffman, Senior Vice President
William R. Gray, Vice President and Director, Book Division
Barbara Lalicki, Director of Children's Publishing
Barbara Brownell, Senior Editor
Mark A. Caraluzzi, Marketing Manager
Vincent P. Ryan, Manufacturing Manager

Library of Congress Catalog Number: 96-068947
ISBN: 0-7922-3446-4

Produced for the National Geographic Society by Weldon Owen Pty Ltd
43 Victoria Street, McMahons Point, NSW 2060, Australia
A member of the Weldon Owen Group of Companies
Sydney • San Francisco

Chairman: Kevin Weldon
President: John Owen
Publisher: Sheena Coupe
Managing Editor: Ariana Klepac
Text Editor: Robert Coupe
Art Director: Sue Burk
Designer: Mark Thacker
Photo Researcher: Anne Ferrier
Production Manager: Caroline Webber

Film production by Mandarin Offset
Printed in Mexico

MY FIRST
POCKET
GUIDE

SEASHORE
LIFE

JENNA KINGHORN

NATIONAL
GEOGRAPHIC
SOCIETY

INTRODUCTION

The seashore is where the ocean meets the land to create beaches, tide pools, caves, and cliffs. Beaches can be made of rocks, coral, ground-up shells, or sand. Tide pools are hollows in rocks that hold water after the tide goes out. The tide is the way that the ocean waves roll into and then out from the shore each day. High tide is when the waves reach the highest point on the beach to cover the tide pools as well as the animals that live there. Low tide is when the waves reach the lowest point on the beach, and the living creatures on the seashore are uncovered. Some animals are difficult to see because their color and shape match their surroundings. Many animals live in cracks, or under seaweed, or buried in the sand, so you need to look hard for them. Never touch an animal you can't identify, because many can sting or pinch. Handle animals gently, and always return them to the spot where you found them.

HOW TO USE THIS BOOK

This book groups together animals that are
related. You will first learn about simple
sponges, then about animals that sting their
prey. Next you'll find different kinds of
shelled animals, such as crabs. Then come
fish, and finally, sea birds. Each spread in
this book helps you identify one kind of
creature. It gives you information about its
size, color, appearance, and behavior. You
can see how long it is by measuring it with
the ruler on the inside of the back cover.
"Where To Find" has a map of North
America that is shaded to show you where
the creature lives, along with a description of
the creature's home. Discover an unusual
fact about the animal in the "Field Notes,"
and see it in its natural environment in the
photograph. If you find a word you do not
know, look it up in the Glossary on page 76.

SPONGE

 The sponges (SPUN-jez) you use at home are probably made in a factory, but animals called sponges grow in the sea. They eat and breathe by sucking water through pores, which are tiny holes in their skin.

WHERE TO FIND:
Look for sponges underwater, on rocks, coral, piers, and other hard objects along the coast.

WHAT TO LOOK FOR:

✳ **SIZE**
A sponge can be as small as a golf ball or as big as a barrel.

✳ **COLOR**
Sponges can be red, orange, yellow, green, blue, or purple.

✳ **BEHAVIOR**
Some sponges make tunnels in shells, coral, and rocks, which they hide in.

✳ **MORE**
If a piece of a sponge breaks off, it may grow into a new sponge.

Look closely and you may see water jetting
out of the large holes in a sponge.

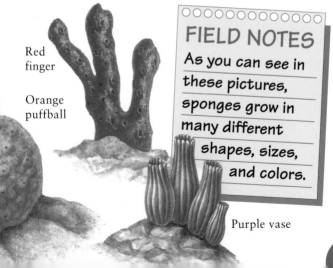

Red
finger

Orange
puffball

Purple vase

FIELD NOTES
As you can see in
these pictures,
sponges grow in
many different
shapes, sizes,
and colors.

ANEMONE

They look like flowers, but anemones (uh-NEM-uh-neez) are animals. They have petal-like, poisonous tentacles that they use to catch and stun small fish and other sea animals that they eat. At low tide, they close up to keep from drying out.

FIELD NOTES

A closed-up anemone has water trapped inside it. If you poke the creature, it will squirt you.

Underwater at high tide, anemones open up like flowers to trap food with their waving tentacles.

WHERE TO FIND:
Anemones stick to rocks under ledges, in cracks, and in caves that are uncovered at low tide.

WHAT TO LOOK FOR:

✳ **SIZE**
Anemones can be as small as nickels or as big as dinner plates.

✳ **COLOR**
They can be many different colors. Their tentacles can be striped or spotted.

✳ **BEHAVIOR**
An anemone moves slowly along the surface of a rock.

✳ **MORE**
Anemones' tentacles are sticky to help them catch prey.

CORAL

Imagine an underwater garden. That's what groups of coral look like. Coral is a collection of tiny animals called polyps (PAHL-uhps). Each polyp builds a stone cup around itself, and all the polyps' cups stick together.

Coral may get very big, but it grows very slowly—less than an inch per year!

WHERE TO FIND:
Most types of coral live in warm, shallow water. Some types live in cold waters off Canada.

WHAT TO LOOK FOR:

✳ SIZE
Each polyp is less than an inch tall, but together they make coral that ranges from 6 inches to 15 feet tall.

✳ COLOR
Coral can be purple, red, orange, yellow, blue, green, or white.

✳ BEHAVIOR
Polyps need sunlit water to live in.

✳ MORE
Polyps have colorful, poisonous tentacles that catch tiny animals drifting by.

FIELD NOTES
Coral comes in many shapes, sizes, and colors. Brain coral looks like a brain.

Brain coral

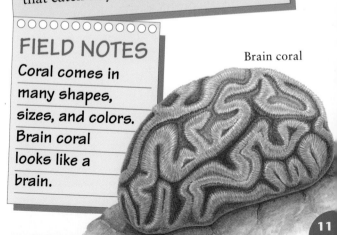

JELLYFISH

Soft and see-through like jelly, a jellyfish has no bones. It has long, stinging tentacles that hang down from its body. It uses these to sting and kill food, such as shrimp, and then drag it into its mouth.

Portuguese man-of-war

FIELD NOTES

Jellyfish, such as the Portuguese man-of-war, can have a very painful sting. Never touch a jellyfish!

Jellyfish do not swim strongly. They drift wherever currents and winds push them.

WHERE TO FIND:
Jellyfish usually live in the open sea, but they are sometimes washed ashore onto beaches.

WHAT TO LOOK FOR:

✳ SIZE
Jellyfish are from a few inches wide to the size of an adult person. Their tentacles can be as long as 100 feet.

✳ COLOR
They come in many different colors.

✳ BEHAVIOR
A jellyfish swims by opening and closing its body, like an umbrella, to push itself through the water.

✳ MORE
A jellyfish's body is almost all water.

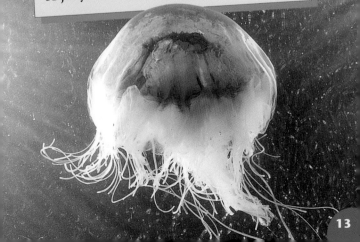

OCTOPUS

 An octopus has a kind of foot that is divided into eight armlike tentacles. It uses these to catch shrimp and crabs, which are its main food. Suckers on each of the tentacles help the octopus to hold onto rocks.

WHERE TO FIND:
Octopuses hide under rocks, in holes, and under plants near the low-tide line off both coasts.

WHAT TO LOOK FOR:

✳ **SIZE**
An octopus can be from a few inches long to 16 feet long.

✳ **COLOR**
An octopus is grayish brown, but it can change color to blend into its background to hide from a predator.

✳ **BEHAVIOR**
A female lays her eggs in a cave.

✳ **MORE**
An octopus has a small, hard shell, like a skeleton, inside its soft body.

An octopus shoots jets of water out of its body to push it through the water.

FIELD NOTES

An octopus squirts out black ink so that a predator cannot see the octopus as it escapes.

SEA SNAIL

Like a garden snail, a sea snail can hide inside its shell if it senses danger. It has a long, rough tongue, like a file, for scraping food off plants and for drilling into shelled animals, like clams, to eat them.

FIELD NOTES

To protect her eggs, a female moon snail binds them with sand into a round, flat mass called a sand collar.

For protection, the moon snail keeps its soft body part almost completely covered by sand.

WHERE TO FIND:

You can find sea snails hunting for food on rocks, plants, and sand, both above and underwater.

WHAT TO LOOK FOR:

✳ SIZE

Sea snails can be as small as your fingertip, or as big as a saucer.

✳ COLOR

They can be different colors, such as black, pink, or orange.

✳ BEHAVIOR

A sea snail wiggles slowly along on a large, slimy kind of foot.

✳ MORE

It sucks in food through its long, tubelike mouth.

PERIWINKLE

A periwinkle (PAIR-ee-WING-kuhl) is a kind of small sea snail with a cone-shaped shell. It has a tongue, called a radula, which is longer than its body. It keeps the radula rolled up inside its shell when it isn't eating.

WHERE TO FIND:
Look for periwinkles, both in and out of water, on rocks, driftwood, seaweeds, and marsh grasses.

WHAT TO LOOK FOR:

✳ **SIZE**
Periwinkles can grow to one inch high.

✳ **COLOR**
They are black, brown, or gray.

✳ **BEHAVIOR**
The periwinkle scrapes algae off rocks and plants with its radula. It has a foot that it wiggles slowly along on.

✳ **MORE**
On grassy shores such as salt marshes, periwinkles climb on seaweed and marsh grasses and eat them.

Periwinkles can survive out of water for many weeks by storing water inside their shells.

19

SLIPPER SHELL

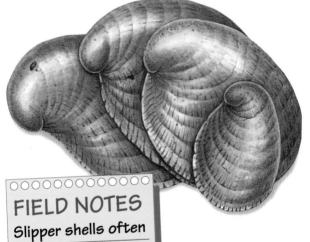

Another type of sea snail, the slipper shell, has a flat, oblong shell. If you hold one upside down, a white shelf that covers part of the shell's opening makes it look like a slipper or a boat.

FIELD NOTES

Slipper shells often climb into stacks. The ones on top are males. The bigger ones underneath are females.

When slipper shells are upside down, it is easy to see why people say they look like slippers.

WHERE TO FIND:
Slipper shells live in shallow water, on rocks, on other shells, and, in the Atlantic, on horseshoe crabs.

WHAT TO LOOK FOR:

✳ SIZE
Slipper shells can grow as long as two inches.

✳ COLOR
They are brown or white. Some have brown or reddish markings.

✳ BEHAVIOR
A female slipper shell keeps her eggs under her shell until they hatch.

✳ MORE
Young slipper shells travel around, but adults stay in one place.

21

WHELK

A whelk (HWELK) is a type of large, meat-eating sea snail. It feeds on clams, oysters, and other shelled animals. A whelk uses its foot and the point of its shell to force open the shells of its prey.

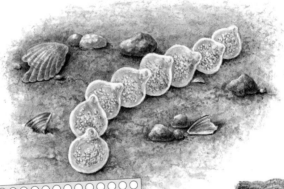

Whelks move around the seafloor looking for living or dead animals to eat.

WHERE TO FIND:
Look for whelks in shallow
water where the floor is
muddy or sandy. Look for
the egg cases on the beach.

WHAT TO LOOK FOR:

✳ **SIZE**
Most whelks are less than 2 inches
long, but some grow to over 16 inches.

✳ **COLOR**
They can be shades of brown, gray, or
yellowish white.

✳ **BEHAVIOR**
They lay their eggs in long strings of egg
cases that often wash up on beaches.

✳ **MORE**
Whelks' shells often have knobs or
pointy spikes on them.

LIMPET

Even in pounding waves, a limpet can cling to a rock. It sticks itself to the rock with a muscular kind of foot. At low tide a limpet seals its shell down against the rock to trap water inside.

FIELD NOTES

The owl limpet pushes barnacles and mussels off rocks. Then algae grows there, which it eats.

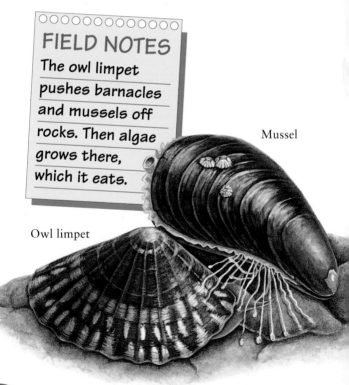

Mussel

Owl limpet

Limpets eat algae and seaweed that they scrape off rocks.

WHERE TO FIND:
Look for limpets in and around tide pools, above and below the water, especially where waves pound.

WHAT TO LOOK FOR:

* **SIZE**
Limpets can be as big as your fingertip or up to five inches long.

* **COLOR**
They are black, brown, white, gray, or a mixture of these colors.

* **BEHAVIOR**
Each limpet has a home base, which is a slight hollow in a rock.

* **MORE**
Some kinds of limpets have smooth shells. Others have ridged shells.

CHITON

A chiton (KITE-uhn) has eight shells that overlap each other. The shells are held together with flesh, called a mantle. If you look underneath a chiton, you can see its round head with a mouth, but the chiton has no eyes.

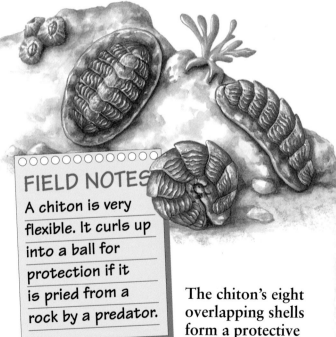

The chiton's eight overlapping shells form a protective coat of armor.

WHERE TO FIND:
Chitons live on and under rocks in tide pools and channels and in other damp areas.

WHAT TO LOOK FOR:

✳ SIZE
Chitons grow from 1 to 13 inches long.

✳ COLOR
They can be many colors, from black or brown to red, pink, or blue.

✳ BEHAVIOR
Most chitons scrape algae from rocks with their long radulas, or tongues. Some filter food out of the water.

✳ MORE
Chitons have a foot that they use to grip tightly to rocks.

27

CLAM

A clam lives in sand or mud. It eats and breathes by sucking in water through tubes of flesh. It moves along slowly on a muscular foot, which it also uses to dig itself into the sand. Its shell is in two halves.

WHERE TO FIND:
You are likely to find clams in shallow water or on tidal mud flats, buried in mud or sand.

WHAT TO LOOK FOR:

✳ SIZE
Most clams grow between three and four inches long.

✳ COLOR
They are usually light gray or white.

✳ BEHAVIOR
Clams burrow quickly into sand or mud to hide from predators.

✳ MORE
Razor and jackknife clams have long, narrow shells. Pismo and surf clams are triangular. Quahogs (KO-hogs) are oval.

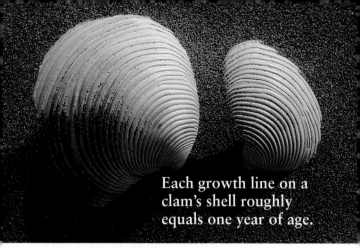

Each growth line on a clam's shell roughly equals one year of age.

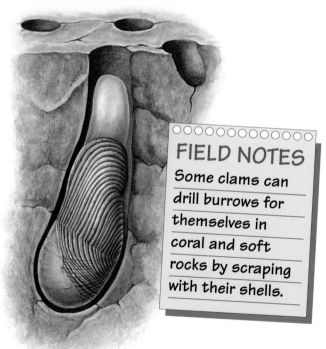

FIELD NOTES

Some clams can drill burrows for themselves in coral and soft rocks by scraping with their shells.

SCALLOP

The two shells of a scallop are shaped like bowls and fit tightly together. They have raised ridges, or ribs, which make them stronger and help protect the scallop's soft body inside.

FIELD NOTES

A scallop pushes itself through the water by quickly clapping its two shells together.

The blue dots are the scallop's light-sensitive eyes, which it uses to sense danger.

WHERE TO FIND:
Scallops live in the sandy mud of shallow waters among eelgrass, or attached to rocks and other hard objects.

WHAT TO LOOK FOR:

✴ SIZE
Most scallops are between one and four inches long.

✴ COLOR
They are white, dark gray, or brown.

✴ BEHAVIOR
A scallop opens its shells to filter food, such as algae, from the water.

✴ MORE
A scallop uses tiny tentacles at the edges of its open shells to sense smells and tastes in the water.

MUSSEL

A mussel's shell is in two halves. When it hatches, a young mussel, called a spat, floats on the water until it settles on a rock. It spends the rest of its life there. Sometimes mussels lie buried in mud.

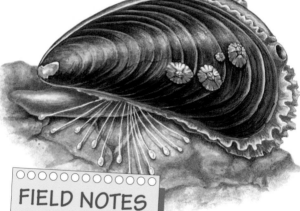

FIELD NOTES

A mussel moves by pushing out anchor threads that stick to rocks. It then pulls itself along on these threads.

At low tide, mussels shut their shells tightly to keep water inside.

WHERE TO FIND:
You may see hundreds of mussels in shallow water, attached to rocks or the supports of piers.

WHAT TO LOOK FOR:

✳ **SIZE**
Mussels can be between one and nine inches long.

✳ **COLOR**
Mussels are black, blue, brown, or gray.

✳ **BEHAVIOR**
They feed by sucking water into their shells and filtering out particles of plant.

✳ **MORE**
They make strong anchor threads that they use to attach themselves to rocks.

OYSTER

 Like mussels, oysters feed mainly on algae by filtering the tiny plants out of the water they suck in. Oysters have round or oval shells. Some shells are smooth, and others are spiny, rippled, or wrinkled.

WHERE TO FIND:
Oysters live in shallow water near the seashore, or where rivers meet the sea, attached to rocks or buried in mud.

WHAT TO LOOK FOR:

✳ SIZE
Oysters grows up to eight inches across.

✳ COLOR
An oyster is grayish or yellowish white, orange, or reddish brown.

✳ BEHAVIOR
When an oyster is a few weeks old, it anchors itself to a rock or another oyster's shell. It never moves again.

✳ MORE
Oysters can change sex, from male to female and back again.

FIELD NOTES

To create a pearl, an oyster coats a sand grain inside its shell with layers of the shell's pearl lining.

Oysters pump water so fast while they filter food, that they make tiny fountains of water.

BARNACLE

Hard plates completely cover and protect the soft bodies of barnacles. These animals spend their lives clustered, head down, in huge numbers on rocks or piers, cemented there by a kind of natural superglue.

When the tide rises, water splashing against these barnacles brings tiny water plants and animals to them to eat.

WHERE TO FIND:
Barnacles cover areas where seawater splashes and pounds on rocks and other hard objects, such as piers.

WHAT TO LOOK FOR:

✳ SIZE
Barnacles can be as small as your fingertip, or as big as six inches wide and three inches high.

✳ COLOR
Barnacles are white to light gray.

✳ BEHAVIOR
Some barnacles grow on boats. Some even grow on whales.

✳ MORE
Some barnacles are shaped like tiny volcanoes.

FIELD NOTES
Barnacles have feathery feet that they use to scoop through the water to catch food.

SHRIMP

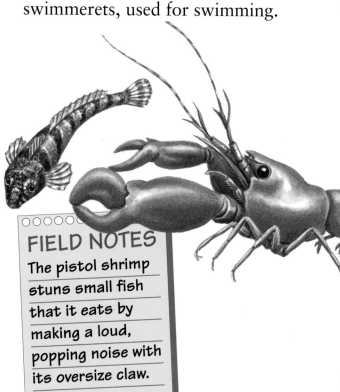

A shrimp's thin shell is like a skeleton outside its body. Shrimp have long legs for walking and gripping, and smaller paddle-shaped back legs, called swimmerets, used for swimming.

FIELD NOTES

The pistol shrimp stuns small fish that it eats by making a loud, popping noise with its oversize claw.

This cleaning shrimp eats tiny animals and plants off of a moray eel.

WHERE TO FIND:
Shrimp live burrowed in mud or sand, or they hide in pools or among anemones' tentacles.

WHAT TO LOOK FOR:

✳ SIZE
Most shrimp are smaller than your thumb, but some grow to a foot long.

✳ COLOR
Shrimp vary from being transparent, or see-through, to being brightly colored.

✳ BEHAVIOR
Cleaning shrimp eat tiny plants and small animals off the skin of fishes.

✳ MORE
Some shrimp have antennae (an-TEN-ee), or feelers, that they use to explore.

CRAB

Like a suit of armor, a crab's shell protects it from attackers. A crab has two claws for holding and tearing food and for fighting. If a crab's claw breaks off, a new one grows back.

FIELD NOTES

When a crab grows too big for its shell, the shell splits and the crab climbs out of it. The crab then grows a new shell.

A crab's eyes are on stalks and can move in all directions.

WHERE TO FIND:
Crabs live along coastlines in cracks and under plants in tide pools, or in burrows in sand.

WHAT TO LOOK FOR:

✳ **SIZE**
Crabs measure from less than one inch across up to ten inches across.

✳ **COLOR**
A crab's shell matches the color of the rocks, plants, or sand where it lives.

✳ **BEHAVIOR**
Some crabs hide by covering themselves with plants and other objects.

✳ **MORE**
A crab walks quickly, moving sideways on its eight back legs.

FIDDLER CRAB

 When the tide is out, large numbers of fiddler crabs crawl over the mud and grass of a salt marsh looking for the remains of dead sea animals and plants to eat. The male has one huge claw.

WHERE TO FIND:
Watch for fiddler crabs near holes in mud flats or in the banks of salt marsh channels.

WHAT TO LOOK FOR:

✳ **SIZE**
Fiddler crabs are up to two inches wide.

✳ **COLOR**
They vary from purple or gray-blue to brown. The male's large claw has brighter markings.

✳ **BEHAVIOR**
When the male waves its claw, it looks a bit like someone playing a fiddle.

✳ **MORE**
If a male fiddler crab loses its large claw, the small claw will grow bigger.

The fiddler crab's big claw looks dangerous, but it is not strong enough to be a weapon.

FIELD NOTES

To attract a mate, a male stands at the entrance to its burrow and waves its large claw.

HERMIT CRAB

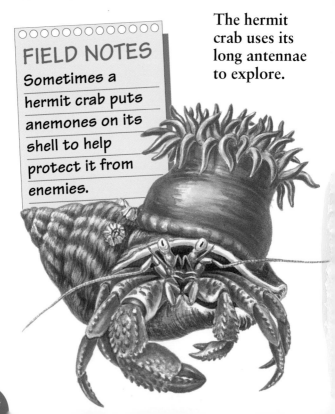

Because it has no shell of its own, a hermit crab lives in an empty sea snail's shell. When frightened, a hermit crab pulls back into the shell, blocking the opening with its claws.

FIELD NOTES

Sometimes a hermit crab puts anemones on its shell to help protect it from enemies.

The hermit crab uses its long antennae to explore.

WHERE TO FIND:
Hermit crabs live in cracks and under plants in rock pools. If you frighten them, they will hide in their shells.

WHAT TO LOOK FOR:

✳ SIZE
Hermit crabs grow to between one and four inches long.

✳ COLOR
They are reddish purple to grayish white. Their claws and legs often have bright markings.

✳ BEHAVIOR
Because it keeps growing, a hermit crab often needs to find a new, bigger shell.

✳ MORE
The right claw is bigger than the left.

HORSESHOE CRAB

 The horseshoe crab looks different from other crabs. It has a hollow, horseshoe-shaped shell on its back, a long tail, and five pairs of legs. Its tail is spiky and looks dangerous, but it is harmless.

WHERE TO FIND:
Horseshoe crabs live in shallow water along the Atlantic coast, and in the Gulf of Mexico.

WHAT TO LOOK FOR:

✳ SIZE
Horseshoe crabs can grow up to two feet long and one foot wide.

✳ COLOR
A horseshoe crab is brownish.

✳ BEHAVIOR
If it is turned upside down, it uses its pointed tail to turn itself over.

✳ MORE
It has no teeth, but it grinds up shelled animals and worms with special plates at the base of its legs, as it walks along.

The horseshoe crab's shell is so tough that it does not mind hitchhikers like these small slipper shells.

SEA STAR

Sea stars, also called starfish, have five or more legs, called rays, that are joined in the center to form a star shape. Underneath the rays are tube feet that are like suction cups. Sea stars use these for gripping things and for moving slowly along rocks.

FIELD NOTES

A sea star wraps its rays around a a clam and uses its tube feet to pull the clam's shells apart.

Sea stars are many different colors and sizes.

WHERE TO FIND:
You can find sea stars in cracks and under plants and rocks in tide pools along both coastlines.

WHAT TO LOOK FOR:

✳ SIZE
Sea stars grow from less than one inch across to three feet across.

✳ COLOR
They can be different colors. Some have patterns.

✳ BEHAVIOR
If a sea star loses a ray, a new ray will grow in its place. The lost ray may grow into a whole new sea star.

✳ MORE
Some sea stars have up to 30 rays!

SEA URCHIN

With many hard spines sticking out of its round body, a sea urchin (ER-chin) looks like a porcupine. It uses these spines to move and to burrow into rocks to make a small cave for hiding in.

FIELD NOTES

A sea urchin moves its spines to point them at something that scares it—like a person's hand.

The spines of the sea urchin hide its shell covered with bumps and holes.

WHERE TO FIND:
Sea urchins often live in large, close groups in tide pools and shallow water along the coastlines.

WHAT TO LOOK FOR:

* **SIZE**
A sea urchin can be as small as a golf ball or as large as a softball.

* **COLOR**
Sea urchins are purple, green, or red.

* **BEHAVIOR**
Using its tube feet, a sea urchin moves half an inch per minute. Using its spines, it moves nearly ten feet per minute.

* **MORE**
A sea urchin has tube feet for gripping food and surfaces and for moving.

SEA CUCUMBER

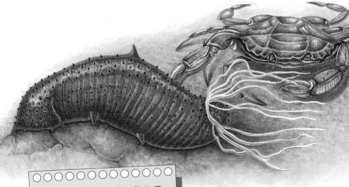

With its long, rounded body, a sea cucumber looks like a cucumber or a giant slug. A sea cucumber has no head. It has a mouth at one end for eating, and a hole at the other for getting rid of wastes.

FIELD NOTES

To escape from an attacker, a sea cucumber shoots out strings of sticky threads into the enemy's face.

A sea cucumber is inflated with seawater, like a water balloon.

Sea cucumbers live underwater on sandy or muddy seafloors, or in crevices and under rocks.

WHAT TO LOOK FOR:

✳ **SIZE**
Sea cucumbers can grow to 19 inches long and 5 inches thick.

✳ **COLOR**
Sea cucumbers are purple, green, red, orange, brown, or black.

✳ **BEHAVIOR**
Feathery tentacles around a sea cucumber's mouth help it to catch food.

✳ **MORE**
It has tube feet that help it move and to cling to rocks.

SAND DOLLAR

Covered with sharp bristles but flat like a silver dollar coin, a sand dollar is a kind of sea urchin. On its back is a flower-shaped pattern of tube feet through which the sand dollar sucks in water.

When sand dollars die, they lose their bristles and become the color of the surrounding sand.

WHERE TO FIND:
Sand dollars live on sandy or muddy seafloors. Dead sand dollars often wash up on beaches.

WHAT TO LOOK FOR:

✳ SIZE
Sand dollars can be as small as dimes or as big as saucers.

✳ COLOR
They are a purplish red color.

✳ BEHAVIOR
Sand dollars eat tiny pieces of dead plants and animals, which they gather with their tube feet.

✳ MORE
A sand dollar's mouth is a small hole on its underside.

FIELD NOTES
A sand dollar uses its short bristles to burrow into the sand and to hide from its enemies.

55

PIPEFISH

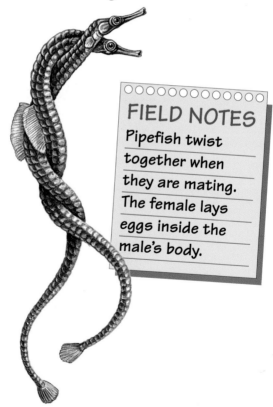

The long, slender pipefish looks like the blades of eelgrass and seaweed that it hides in. It swims with its head up and tail down, and sucks in small fishes and other sea animals through its small mouth.

FIELD NOTES

Pipefish twist together when they are mating. The female lays eggs inside the male's body.

The pipefish has hard, armorlike plates that protect it from predators.

WHERE TO FIND:
Pipefish live in the waters off the Pacific coast, Atlantic coast, and Gulf Coast.

WHAT TO LOOK FOR:

✳ SIZE
Pipefish grow from three inches up to four feet long.

✳ COLOR
Most pipefish are plain green or brown, but some are striped.

✳ BEHAVIOR
The male keeps eggs in a slit in his body until the young hatch. Babies may go back into this slit if they are scared.

✳ MORE
Pipefish often hide to escape predators.

SEA HORSE

 The sea horse is a fish with a head shaped like a horse's, plates of armor like an armadillo's, and a tail like a monkey's. It swims with its head up and its tail down. The sea horse's armor plates protect it against predators.

WHERE TO FIND:
Sea horses live among water plants near southern California and Mexico and along the Atlantic and Gulf coasts.

WHAT TO LOOK FOR:

* SIZE
Sea horses grow between four inches and one foot long.

* COLOR
Sea horses are gray, brown, black, green, yellow-orange. Some have spots.

* BEHAVIOR
A sea horse wraps its tail around plants, or another sea horse, to anchor itself.

* MORE
The female sea horse lays her eggs in a pouch on the male's belly.

The sea horse is often hard to see because it blends into the color of its background.

FIELD NOTES

The male keeps the female's eggs in a pouch on his belly until the young hatch.

SCULPIN

Dark blotches all over its body and hard-to-see, spiky fins help keep this fish hidden from predators as it darts quickly from one hiding place to another in the tide pools where it lives.

FIELD NOTES

When hiding from predators, sculpins change color and blend into the background.

It's hard to see a sculpin against its background unless it moves.

WHERE TO FIND:

Look for sculpins hiding under seaweed and behind rocks in tide pools.

WHAT TO LOOK FOR:

✳ SIZE
Sculpins grow between two and four inches long.

✳ COLOR
They can be green, reddish brown, pink, or purple, with darker spots.

✳ BEHAVIOR
Some sculpins always return to the same "home" pool after they swim out at high tide to look for food.

✳ MORE
They feed on tiny, shelled sea animals.

EEL

Eels are long, thin fish. Like snakes slithering over land, eels swim by moving their ribbonlike bodies from side to side. They can also swim backward in this way. They hunt at night and hide by day.

A moray eel has one long fin that runs along its back.

WHERE TO FIND:
Eels live in the warm waters of the southern coasts, in cracks and caves in rocks and among corals.

WHAT TO LOOK FOR:

✳ SIZE
Eels grow up to five feet long.

✳ COLOR
They can be yellow, green, gray, or brown. Some have brown spots.

✳ BEHAVIOR
From their hiding places in cracks and caves, eels ambush octopus, fish, crabs, and other similar prey.

✳ MORE
Eels twist and turn easily because they have up to 100 bones in their backbones.

GULL

There are many different kinds of gulls, and they are all scavengers. This means that instead of hunting live prey, these birds eat dead animals or try to steal food from other birds and animals.

FIELD NOTES

To open a shellfish to eat, a gull keeps dropping the shell on the ground from high in the air until it breaks open.

Gulls usually face into the wind when they are standing or sitting.

WHERE TO FIND:
Look for gulls bobbing on the waves, sitting on docks, flying overhead, or walking along the beach.

WHAT TO LOOK FOR:

❋ SIZE
Gulls can be 14 to 30 inches long and have wingspans from 3 to 6 feet.

❋ COLOR
Gulls are mostly gray and white with black markings.

❋ BEHAVIOR
Gulls are noisy and fight each other for food. Baby gulls peck at the red spot on a parent's beak to beg for food.

❋ MORE
Gulls' feet are webbed for swimming.

PUFFIN

With its white breast, orange legs and feet, and colorful beak, a puffin is easy to recognize. Puffins spend most of the year at sea, but they come back to land in spring to breed. They nest on rocky cliffs.

Puffins nest in well-protected places like small, rocky islands or high cliffs.

WHERE TO FIND:
Look for puffins guarding the openings to their burrows along sea cliffs and on rocky islands.

WHAT TO LOOK FOR:

✷ **SIZE**
Puffins are 12 to 15 inches long.

✷ **COLOR**
They are black and white with white faces and orange and yellow bills that turn orange and red at breeding time.

✷ **BEHAVIOR**
Puffins swim on the ocean's surface and dive underwater to catch small fish, eels, squid, and other prey.

✷ **MORE**
Female puffins lay only one egg a year.

FIELD NOTES
The tufted puffin is all black except for its white face. It gets its name from the long, yellow tufts on its head.

Tufted puffin

PELICAN

 The white pelican swims on the water's surface and dips its head underwater to catch fish to eat. The brown pelican spots a fish in the water while it is flying high in the air. It then swoops down onto the fish.

WHERE TO FIND:
Pelicans fly low over the water in V-shaped flocks. They swim in harbors near fishing boats.

WHAT TO LOOK FOR:

✻ SIZE
A pelican is four to five feet long.

✻ COLOR
Pelicans are white or grayish brown, with orange or brownish white bills.

✻ BEHAVIOR
Pelicans are graceful fliers and can glide through the air in strong breezes, without flapping their wings.

✻ MORE
The white pelican grows a bump on its bill during breeding season.

The brown pelican's head is yellow and black during the breeding season.

FIELD NOTES

A pelican's bill has a pouch like a fishing net. It uses it to scoop up fish, before swallowing them.

White pelican

HERON

A heron is a long-legged, long-necked wading bird that catches fish and other food in shallow water. It has long toes that help it to grip onto branches when it perches and nests in trees.

Great blue heron

FIELD NOTES

The great blue heron flies with its neck curled back so that its head rests on its shoulders.

The heron stands as still as a statue, waiting for its prey to come near. Then it strikes.

WHERE TO FIND:

Look for herons wading in salt marshes and tide pools—wherever the water is shallow and still.

WHAT TO LOOK FOR:

✳ **SIZE**
Herons are two to four feet long.

✳ **COLOR**
They are blue-gray, green, or brown, with white and black markings.

✳ **BEHAVIOR**
Herons swallow their food while it is still alive. They eat fish and frogs.

✳ **MORE**
Herons rake their feathers with the comblike middle toes on their feet.

71

CORMORANT

A cormorant (COR-muh-ruhnt) sometimes eats so many fish that it is almost too heavy to fly. The cormorant then runs along the water's surface, flapping its wings wildly until it takes off.

Cormorants are strong swimmers because of their large, webbed feet.

WHERE TO FIND:
Cormorants stay close to the rocky ledges and cliffs where they roost. They swim above and below the water.

WHAT TO LOOK FOR:

✱ SIZE
A cormorant is two to three feet long.

✱ COLOR
It is black or blackish green, often with a blue, red, orange, or white patch on its face or throat.

✱ BEHAVIOR
A cormorant swims underwater, using its wings as well as its webbed feet.

✱ MORE
A hook at the tip of its bill helps it to keep hold of wriggling fish.

FIELD NOTES
To dry their wet feathers, cormorants stand on rocks with their wings spread out wide.

73

SANDERLING

Sanderlings (SAN-der-lingz) are from a family of birds called sandpipers. They have rounded bodies and long, sticklike legs. They run quickly with a jerky motion, bending down to snatch up tiny animals from the sand to eat.

FIELD NOTES

Sanderlings try to grab a meal of shellfish at the water's edge before the surf rushes in.

The sanderling pokes its thin bill into the sand to find food.

WHERE TO FIND:
Look for sanderlings on sandy beaches where the surf is always washing in and out.

WHAT TO LOOK FOR:

✳ **SIZE**
A sanderling is up to eight inches long.

✳ **COLOR**
Its feathers are light gray in winter and rusty brown in summer. It has a white belly and dark legs.

✳ **BEHAVIOR**
A sanderling makes its nest in a moss-lined hollow in the ground.

✳ **MORE**
It uses its long, black bill to explore the sand for shellfish and crabs to eat.

GLOSSARY

Abdomen The back section of the body.

Acid A strong chemical that burns or dissolves objects it touches.

Algae (AL-gee) Plants that live in the water and have no roots, leaves, or stems.

Eelgrass A plant with leaves like ribbons that grows in shallow water.

Limestone Rock made from the ancient shells and bones of dead sea animals.

Marsh grasses Grasses growing in an area that is sometimes flooded.

Mate When an adult male and female come together to produce young.

Mud flat A flat, muddy area in a salt marsh that is uncovered at low tide.

Parasite An animal or plant that lives in or on another animal and takes its food from that body.

Particle A tiny piece.

Predator Any creature that hunts other creatures for food.

Prey Any creature that is hunted by other creatures for food.

Salt marsh An area of low ground partly or completely covered by the ocean at high tide.

Salt marsh channels Streams or creeks found in salt marshes.

Seaweed A type of algae that grows in saltwater.

Suckers Suction cups on an octopus's tentacles that it uses for gripping things.

Tentacles The long, thin feelers that an octopus and some other sea creatures use for grasping and feeding.

Tide During the day the ocean rolls onto and away from the beach. When the waves roll to the lowest point on the beach, that is "low tide." When they roll to the highest point, it is "high tide."

Tide pool A small hollow in rock or coral that is left filled with water at low tide.

Tube feet Suction cups on a sea creature such as a starfish, sea urchin, or sea cucumber, that it uses to grasp things.

Wastes Food material that is not used by the body for fuel. It is sent out of the body.

INDEX OF
SEASHORE LIFE

ABOUT THE CONSULTANT

Jenna Kinghorn graduated Summa Cum Laude from Beloit College (Beloit, Wisconsin) with a B.A. in Science Writing. She previously worked for the Mendocino Headlands State Park in Mendocino, California, and Ano Neuvo State Reserve in Davenport, California, writing, creating exhibits, leading hikes, and teaching school children and other visitors about coastal habitats and wildlife. She has enjoyed studying tide pools and seashore life since childhood, and frequently scuba dives near her home on the coast of northern California.

PHOTOGRAPHIC CREDITS